The
Shape
of the
Keyhole

The
Shape
of the
Keyhole

Denise Bergman

Black
Lawrence
Press

Black
Lawrence
Press

www.blacklawrence.com

Executive Editor: Diane Goettel
Book Design: Amy Freels
Cover Design: Zoe Norvell

Copyright © Denise Bergman 2020
ISBN: 978-1-62557-824-2

Published 2020 by Black Lawrence Press.
Printed in the United States.

For Gerry

Contents

In 1650 in Cambridge, Massachusetts, a woman was hanged for "bewitching to death" her friend's child.

The single, and remarkably brief, historical account includes this accusation by the child's nurse: "She did make much of the child, and then the child was well, but quickly changed its color and dyed in a few hours."

Almost immediately after the woman was hanged—denying her guilt to the end—it was discovered that the child died because the nurse brought him with her into the woods in the freezing cold so she could be with her secret lover.

Day One

The one in the constable's robe taps
knuckles on her door

fingers fisted white around bone,
wrist the knocker hinge

Taps his knuckles

She empties the wash bucket,
walks 'round to the front,
sees the back of the man—*yes?*

Bucket clanks, rolls to a rock

stops

A lit fuse, his knuckle fist

No warning, the knock not a warning

The knock a command

A sentence

Read it forward, in reverse

Subject verb ignite verb subject

The end starts here

---

indecipherable command the knock she doesn't know the end
encoded in the beginning
—codebreakers deep asleep even awake if ever awake which key

the shape of the keyhole is the shape of the key

He knocked he could have barged in

Yes?
Impatient

she doesn't recognize him,
expected the neighbor needed eggs

Yes? clipped,
impatient

Lye coats her hands

Yes?

His knuckles retrieve a pulse,
disappear like ancient turtles into his cuff

She has only time to fetch her cape

Autopsy, *autopsia*, "see for oneself"
blue the boy's lips fingers toes ears nose

The cold had stuck in the red gum, they said,
the red gum come out upon him

Felled by ignorance, shrunken by pride,
the examiners
stopped looking for why

blamed her as their disguise

mistake
missed stake mistaken wrongly taken
not for the taking take
stakes high stakes

Between knuckles and their echo
a flash flood

dislodged sediment, fragmented scenes,
churned up voices

She had burped her friend's newborn,
cradled him, tickled him

rhymes singsongs, taught him
playful disobedience

to roll down a hill,
lure a gopher with a treenut

Flash flood presses her lungs' bellows—

to never hear, touch,
see him again—breathe!

Sudden surge then the flood recedes,
still, no turning around

She had held tight her friend's shoulders
before the baby's head crowned

lifted the placenta from the midwife's hands

suggested his name

Who is she

who is she not, that they will hoist her

before
(as she herself would say) double-checking

Who, that no one

saddles a horse,
gallops to the dead boy's mother

asks

Fear awakens fear

Slipping on a crisp of ice, stepping on a fiddlehead

Falling off the roof

Standing too tall, appearing too upright

Loving, letting loose, making mistakes unbeknownst to her

Stumbling on the street

Fear of no fear, fear of a dozen fears

Eggs in a pyramid, forgetting to cross your fingers

Being visible, invisible

Wrong place

Too late, too early

On time

Bobbing-yes heads and glares
sideways airs

Her, her—
she killed that boy,
her

she
herself she did

Told retold:

Not I
I could not would not am not
can't imagine
wielding lightning-rod
venom
on a boy's pink cheek,
unyielding power

for what—for show
or did she lose control

oh, if I had her
hidden
life-ending force

would I

Why does no one ask why

she killed a child
would want to kill
a child
that child

could she not stop herself

her demons
have outgrown their skins

Told retold:

She and the boy built a nest
lined with juniper
for a broken day-old warbler

---

nesting on a low branch the warbler
its eyes too young to see
in the vacant woods
in the well-tracked woods blind deaf
woods of lovers' trysts and secret
masturbations, woods of gold
coins buried under rocks covered in dead leaves
woods too distracted to notice a woman and child soothing
a bird's
trembling head
wishing it future
and flight

Told retold:

She tickled my fevered baby,
he smiled, then laughed

    I called her "friend," oh! what have I done,
    what have I—
    oh! they'll call me witch

Scrub your hands, scrub away her touch,
scrub anything she touched

    But what of her pie pan half-empty

Her pear tree leans over my raspberries,
they shelter in its shade,
sparrows filled with berries peck at her ripe pears,
she ate them anyway

    Never complained

She planted beans in oak shade just, she said, to see

    She and the boy built a small stream dam
    Oh! why did she tell me

A dam stops the river's flow

Featureless night
indistinct

not like but not unlike all others

Pail kicked by a cow
Crickets, bullfrog

A fox is shot

She fumbles for a window,
squints through the jail bars for a light

reaches for a candle, a match

stock-still listens for a voice
to answer the shouting in her head

Gropes for a wall to lean against

Prays for something
anything
familiar to appear

Nurse Accuses

Little pink fingers blue
frozen red fire
toes nose
grape-purple eyelids
lips too cracked
to cry

He shook like a rattle gourd
I clapped his ears
to block the witch's curse
but she snuck in and stole him
from himself

his neck twisted his head
his limbs
darted from her pitch-dark eyes
he was guarding
his soul, every child's instinct, I know
(I know children)

She lured him with her familiar
sweetness, tickled
her hex into his skin, lifted
and swung him
around—
caught in her conjure he laughed
child that he was

Hide-and-seek, pick-up-sticks,
her intention
disguised in leaves they plucked and threw
in the river, in twigs
they floated downstream, her evil
in her still-warm bread

Not for me to say
why she did but she did
bewitch him
I fed him, dressed him
and when I left him on her lap his skin
was his mother's bright pink
if a bit chapped
and somewhat dry

the shape of the keyhole is the shape of the key
aligned in the slot clockwise lock
or counterintuitive left
the hole rough steel forged
what's to figure out
the keyhole adapts to the teeth of the key
it's rudimentary—insert and turn

the keyhole shapes the key the key shapes the keyhole
the key is the voice the keyhole the ear

What If Instead

She begs truth to join her, sit down,
pour a cup of tea
and truth pulls up a chair

Townsfolk say *we'll listen* and listen,
hear, hear her,
squeeze into the spot
where judgment and reason
intersect

The nurse overtakes all that holds her hostage
yells, *I was wrong,* loud and in time

With wide strides women run to the courtroom,
forget fear and hesitation, barge in

Truth tries on history's spectacles,
discovers the multiple views in its reach

Multiple views, the mirage fades

Multiple voices, the loudest fades

The cymbal clash, crescendo crash
obscured by the fiddler retuning his strings

Against prediction
Nightmare loses the race

Day Two

Wide shoulder narrow shoulder tall short
standing sitting fat thin

Plank benches sink
under the sweat-stink sea's rising tide

Can't-wait up-and-down knees
pump bounce jiggle

The crescendo a tease

The buzz—
then silence, *ORDER, SILENCE*

Silence snaps its leather whip

Men turn in one direction

Benches packed as pews

Outside the door, unsure, women pace circles

Fresh washed bonnets, button-up boots

Palms on children's heads, over children's mouths

Shoving to hear the last word first

Pacing circles, ovals, spirals, spiraling

Eager to hear what they're eager to hear

Shoving through their fear

Bobble heads high

jurymen proud to be picked
know what they are told they know

decide
decisive decisions

no need to listen—
listen to what?

Nothing can be said
No one says the nothing

---

jurymen con-jury men conjurymen
stir the cauldron's simple spell
toss in some this some that and chant
while fumes rise smoke blinds
the conjurymen's eyes

Butcher in the jury box
twists to escape her witch eyes

Baker in the front row spits a gargled wad

Preacher shoots her with his trigger finger,
pop with his tongue

Farmer steps out the door,
signals his wife to horse-up the wagon,
go home, milk the cows

Constable boasts his call

Blacksmith's boy sneaks up and slaps her

Fear like smokehouse fire fills her loins

In lieu of a gavel the judge's flat open hand
and when that fails
two hands then two fists

In lieu of sweets and pie, in lieu of boredom,
in lieu of logic

From up high he *bestows* their longed-for
vengeful desire—

The verdict a string of abacus pearls
to count a woman's days

Pearls, links of a fine gold chain,
a clasp even a child can open and close

count a woman's days account for account to
start the count countdown count down
be accountable careful accounting
uncountable unable to count be counted
closed account open account
trusted account
count the uncountable count the uncounted
recount

Word freed from suspension

falls on famished laps

A present to unwrap

Concise two-syllable continuous
repeated sound

ending before it began

first the finish then the start

Pieces of her torn apart
tumble too—

upright is upsidedown,
floor is sky

the fragmented horizon line
vanishes

first the finish then the start
—a rattlesnake swallowing its tail

Scars pocks rashes scarves caps hats,
she scours the courtroom for her husband's face,
for anyone not yet unfamiliar

Searches, but the word before her,
too huge to see behind,
grabs her, tucks her in its breastpocket
over its heart

though the word has no heart

Nurse Recounts to Herself

Home, I
swept through the door
I'd left ajar
(prepared always)
shoes outside the threshold
I lay the boy on his bed
cleaned my boots
tucked the quilt
around the boy with a 1–2–3
back to sleep
but in a whisper, the dog
was wrestling a dream, the boy's
father coughed, mother
rustled, I heated
water to thaw my frozen feet

Yes the boy
was fine—just
ice-gritted mud on his arms
and legs
and his pants and jacket
wet when, home,
the snow in his cuffs
melted

Days Three Four Five Six

Massachusetts Body of Liberties #44: No man [*sic*] condemned
to die shall be put to death within four days next after his [*sic*]
condemnation

—

she begs notice   begs not to be noticed   keep away   step so close
the fear in her breath mists your face   scintillates   hubbub thrill
excitement dizzy spinning chasing   tag you're it   but you're not
it   not her

she's too shocked to be shamed   too shamed to be in shock

she is concentric's center and its widest ring   ripple's cause and
reverberation   the thrown stone's plunk swallowed by silence
she is not the first centricity first to be hanged first innocence
not the last

wagons hobble home   sun constructs a crimson wall   her skin
shivers bones quake   breath an incidental

—

name your obedient dog Verdict   *heel* Verdict *heel*   name a feral
tabby Guilty   mauled mouse in its paws chewed feather whiskers
name a flighty songbird Prisoner   name the ant forever hauling
crumbs Mighty

—

(he [husband]:) my brown eyes two yoked oxen steered straight
ahead   what color her eyes blue?   reins gripped tight   road
pitted and gullied   her eyes hazel?   our supper table too narrow

for talk   in bed my palm turned from hers   when I watched her
pluck weeds from beans I might say your bonnet has untied   her
fingernails bitten toenails crusted   left front tooth chipped and if
she laughed her dogtooth guarded an unapologetic black hole   I
looked when she wasn't looking

(he:) she insisted the ocean was salt   my shoulder freckles night's
constellation fallen into day   wished no star to shatter   she
shattered   I'm not glue   she said no star hangs in the sky alone
at night I smell the ocean

—

neck crooked head cocked   ear free to hear   again   the omitted
not   not broke yesterday to pieces   three fingers under her
jawbone to the left of her chin the vein pulses inside outside her
skin   she tosses her head back and forth   swivels it back and
forth   tosses   swivels   head face eyes   she shuts shuts out her
eyes   her neck flops her chin to her chest

she was the one who always double checked   bucket centered
under the udder   laundry clipped secure to the line   hands
open to catch what came at her   palms wide to break a fall block
danger

—

who doubts whom   what   who doubts why

(he:) nothing's impossible   a spasm in a witch's arm
uncontrolled control   renegade lack of faith   call me scoundrel
I doubt her   quiet deferential her   loyal to me her   wife her
reliable

—

Nightmare won the race   practiced running in the dark
memorized treeroots potholes   pre-envisioned the obstacles
could run the race in its sleep   Nightmare yanked her arm
tugged her wrist   shouldered her off the track

—

(he:) caustic lie spit it out   spatter the acid back in their faces
deface the face of their accusation   I know better   I'll be chased
out of town never to see again the ghost of the wife I'll never see
again   I'll be branded   accomplice pleader   worse   the crazed
man who calls the impossible impossible

—

tethered legs windmill arms   *get away keep away*   she is the
center of concentric circles widening   source of concentric   the
stone skipped on a diurnal pond   rock rolled down a riverbank's
decline   *keep away*   ripples chase you   *avoid her*   avoid the
contagion even her husband won't risk   she is wrong place wrong
time infection plague epicenter   vaccinate inoculate stay away

—

Nightmare hoists its trophy chest-high   people shower the
braggart with their eyes   bugles confetti the celebration wakes
her   wrestles her back to sleep   shouts into her face   wrestles
her to sleep

—

chained to jailhouse shadow   four days will leave no clutter
no untidy loose ends   adults muzzle children's questions   tear
question into eight letters kick them aside so innocence doesn't
trip   pieces of her ride away on wind

the endless day is too short the little life left too long   bitterness
plaques her teeth   her tongue trawls the pink of her palate for
respite   humidity pounds her temples   she fills the hole she has
become with her transparency

(she:) my tongue will dangle   lips flop   mouth freeze in a retch
when they take me down   who will take me down   who will
tuck my tongue back in

she thinks says to no one: another day   kicks the hours'
desiccated stalks into a furrow with her shoe   buries a runaway
acorn with clumped dirt

—

husband thinks says to no one: I can stand with her   but he can't
his steps will trace back to him   he is losing thought   his voice
has lost propulsion   he squints at her wavering body   shadow
afar is substance   substance close up is shadow   who comes
close stays away

—

she'll pay the price the minister says   cobbler calls it the cost
minister cobbler blacksmith   she'll pay   a midwife turns a
future head-first

—

husband can't unmask his face   pluck off the guise like goose
feathers   (he:) oh had she not visited the boy that day   had she
not   that day

—

Nightmare won the race   panting sweating hands wildly waving
victory   spectators jump clap cheer   jeer at justice plodding laps
behind limping out of sight behind never to cross the finish line
some nightmares run faster barefoot   some in shoes   some on
dirt   this one on a flat paved track

—

sunrise she waits to fall asleep as if night were minutes ahead
peers at the ceiling   time is the seesaw fulcrum's two ends
weighted

town awakens with an ear-piercing yawn   church bells   a
mother's call to supper   wretched starving cats

husband tilling the winter-hard ground reconsiders walking
towards her

she says: if you stand behind me you're next in line

—

let the end begin the beginning end   done won't be undone
why wait   she thinks: another day   imagines trudging up the
hill   stumbling   fulfilling the teardrop rope stretching the loop
rehearses the goodbye she'll whisper to herself   to whom else
to no one else   to sparrows hunkering down expecting a storm
to the woodpecker drilling the branch hungry determined
desperate

time aches for an execution   its prickly heat creeps up her neck
the endless day is too long she thinks   her little life left too short

—

surrounding *moment* is *momentum*   spiraling down a funnel
spout   rushing to the river where a woman is stolen by current
to the well where a girl at the bottom apologizes for her worth
to the courthouse where one word ends a life   in *momentum*
is *moment*   one link in a long chain   is *moments* plucked
scrambled one-at-a-time   inside *moment momentum* agitates
to be unleashed

—

(she:) I did his doing his doing got done   heaped buckets so no
berries bled   resewed his cuffs to sleeves in invisible stitches
strangled geese   scraped tendons from the chopping block
baked the pies he brought the young widow

mrs they call me but my mother named me before the wide sea
yanked free from the dock before I waved to the memory of me in
her arms   waves washed away waves

I talk to my self   my mother said a woman talks to her self—dear
dear diary self it's me I am I am   but soon no longer   and never
more of a name than his mrs

whitecaps swells crests   at the ship rail my name clutched me
but gales threw my name overboard and having never known the
sea I never learned to swim

even if I had jumped in and kept my name afloat—how with my
little breath left could I have refilled its lungs

now no name but his wraps me and barely   a weighty moth-
eaten shawl

—

word weighted in script nailed to the courthouse door rattles   as
if paper could rattle   or papyrus wood shingle or cowhide

conjuring the death of a baby   illogic's preposterous collarless suit
too skin-tight to undress

conjury con jury conned jury   one twelve-man-wide mouth
enunciates   lips shape the *guil-*   tongue and teeth the *-ty*

—

soon her head will squeeze through the noose loop rope twisted
by law a uniform number of times   hemp needles will welt
her cheek more red than shame more red than terror   her jaw
a bleeding crosshatch   ears pinned back   chin aligned in its
assigned position on the precipice

—

Massachusetts Body of Liberties #47: No man [*sic*] shall be put
to death without the testimony of two or three witnesses or that
which is equivalent thereunto

one: Nurse, who painted-in her quick-drawn outlines with
opacity

two: Silence, who inherited its loud acquiescence

three: Nightmare, who led the race from the get-go and never
relayed the baton

—

(he:) if I were the day or if the day were mine   you ask   I see the
hours left but can't   and you can't

counter erase nullify   three witnesses testified

—

Nightmare charms all spectators   spectacle spectacular   people travel days to cheer their boy on   Nightmare sweats a torrent and spectators wipe its forehead with their sleeves

Silence snatches the best view of the finishline   hoards the seat governor's government seat   Silence fixed the race and bets on the victor

Silence augurs its power   a hunched wizard with a long stick stirring a boiling cauldron rendering fear

Day Seven

Faces beam, string-her-up eyes,
drip-snot noses, chapped grin lips—
hang her high

Rope twisted seven times knotted twelve,
length to spare

A tom squawks in the distance
Hens defy the fence
A man who didn't come early
took some minutes to wrangle his fowl

A girl whispers to her cousin, *I know her*

The minister hallelujahs, pounds his little book
thud thud, leather to palm

A woman turns beet red as if choking

If I were there would I be there

She straightens her skirt

Hill, sky framed in elm branches,
360° stage, a place

A hill, a view, a stage, spectators, actors

Whose eyes are on her, who is aghast,
for whom is this a party

She looks

If I were there would I be there, if I were there
would I catch her eye

Tugged pulled up the midday hill, handled

Her bootlaces peck the grass

She is led and she trudges on leaden feet
She is pulled by an end

Rowdy circle, the crowd,
and a circle and a circle around that

She will swing in all directions

Some will notice her eyes, some her open palms

Small body, small platform

Slim statue on ridicule's wide pedestal

They tear at her
like crust from bread's warm center

Crumbs where she once stood

Husband's voice hides in a swallow's throat
deep in a cliff wall cave

No room to turn around, not now

At least *now* will soon be *after*

She is walking up the hill accompanied
unaccompanied
by a man she doesn't know

accompanied by her familiar limp
unaccompanied by her hobble

Husband thinks:
How is it

I didn't lie down in the path,
block the path

muzzle with my palms my silence,
shout *no, no! hell no!*
even in church, *hell no!*

How is it, when
they feigned a witch a reason

I didn't
feign reason back

Husband says to himself:
What about

me, dragging my dislodged heart
too, by a rope

The crowd parts,
snaps fingers, *get out of here, get!*

Only last week
leaning on the fence, chuckling:
that one's twice-told story,
this one's lame joke

and at the long table,
the minister handed *me* the knife
to slice the bread

She stumbles, sees him
confused in the mutilated landscape

rubs
her disbelieving eyes

Her head in the teardrop loop

fulfills the loop

Rope, a tug is all that's left

After, where will they take her,
on whose shoulder to what cart with what horse

With whose sharpened spade
are witches buried

The cobbler's sock clumps under the ball of his foot

The mayor's wife ignores her painful time-of-month

An Adam's apple throbs, a forehead drips, a baby sleeps

The butcher's chin drapes his collar,
his collar is his choker but he is not choking
The butcher, who catches blood's gravity in a pail

Husband shuts his eyes, trembles, husband trembles,
cries but lets no one hear,
cries but no one listens, braces, stiffens—
what's next

Inside the crowd alone,
the circle around him widens

Stand up, for once stand up
you, who own her name, her one recorded name

Her him
who yourself won't be hanging from the tree
feet swinging

You, her him
who'll miss his mrs

for better for worse—
or did you decide otherwise

Her eyes—hooded unhooded—are open

Hemp's jagged needles burn a welt on her jaw

Her last word sticks, is stuck in her throat

Her first word *mama*, her last word *no*, her last word *no*
A sentence between *mama* and *no*

He who took her down
whispered in her ear

Whispered,
dismantled her, took her down

Whispered what?

Nurse Confesses

I wouldn't hurt a fly, I watch
its tiny mandibles grind as if scraping
meat from bone
jaw jaw
or the fly on my breast in bed
I pretend it's
his (I won't say whose) fingers
wandering my curves

I brought the boy with me
times and times
many times
but this time the cold
blued his limbs and face, locked open
his frosted eyes

this once only
and I was
cold too, naked to the boy looking
up from the ground
naked to (I won't say who)
then I dressed
and lifted the boy to my chest
and backstepped home
I wouldn't hurt a fly, or myself,
won't let
myself be hurt

a mrs in the record of convictions

first name simply mrs

the only no-first-name listed

in the column "found guilty"
found guilty

in a hasty quote-unquote trial

too, in the record
no recorded day or month

even the year a question

Notes:

Quote on page 1 from Rev. John Hale's *A Modest Enquiry into the Nature of Witchcraft, etc.*, published in 1702, pp. 18–19.

The *Massachusetts Body of Liberties*, published in 1641, is the first legal code established by European colonists in New England and was composed of a list of liberties, rather than restrictions, and intended for use as guidance for the General Court of the time.

Photo: Sarah Boyer

Denise Bergman is the author of four other books of poetry. *Three Hands None* (Black Lawrence Press, 2019) delves into the night forty years ago when the author was attacked in her bed by a stranger. *A Woman in Pieces Crossed a Sea* centers on the making and endurance of "symbol" in the Statue of Liberty. *The Telling* is a book-length poem generated by a relative's one-sentence secret about her escape as a refugee. *Seeing Annie Sullivan* is based on the early life of Helen Keller's teacher.